199 Terribly Good
DAD JOKES

Witty, Funny and Damn Right Awful!

Written By:

Mike Gaffy

Mike Gaffy

199 Terribly Good Dad Jokes, Witty, Funny and Damn Right Awful!

Copyright 2018

Self-published, Gaffy Books

Gaffy Books

GaffyJokes.com

mike@gaffyjokes.com

This is a work of fiction.

Names, characters, businesses, places, events and incidents are either the products of the author's imagination or used in a fictitious manner.

Any resemblance to actual persons, living or dead, or actual events is purely coincidental.

Table of Contents

Bonus!

Get This Free Joke Book!

Hilarious jokes to make you laugh your head off!

Visit The Link Below!

Why you should read this book

Dads are at times awkward, weird and strange. But sometimes they can be funny too. You know, those moments when they embarrass you with their cringe-worthy wit that further alienate you from your friends or partner. Ah, great times.

Dads try to stay on top of the latest trends and look "mainstream" yet don't know that sending game requests on Facebook is social suicide.

Dad jokes are the cheesiest in the world and dads use their ability of bad timing to great effect. Sometimes you don't know whether to laugh or cry or both. Most dad jokes end up with the annoyed response "Daaaad!"

The main difference between bad jokes and dad jokes is simply the first letter. So, without further ado, here is a collection of the greatest worst dad jokes out there.

Chapter One
The Family and Advice for a Son

Son: "Why do you always wear that ridiculous Hawaiian shirt?"

Dad: "So people know I'm your dad."

Mom: "Where did you hide the kids' presents?"

Dad: "The last place they would look: on the roof."

Mom: "This turkey is hard to stuff"

Dad: "Not heard you say that in a while."

A son goes to hug his dad but accidently steps on his toes.

Son: "Sorry, I didn't mean to walk on your feet."

Dad: "That's ok; I walk on them all day."

A dad is driving her daughter and her date to the prom. As the daughter gets out, dad asks the date to stay for the 'dad talk'.

Dad: "You got protection?"

Date: "You mean condoms?"

Dad: "I mean a flare gun."

Daughter: "Dad, can you give me a ride into town?"

Dad: "I can give you change for the bus."

A son and his dad are in different rooms of their house. Suddenly, the son gets a Skype call from his dad telling him to come into the room. The son enters the room and asks "What's up?" His dad to replies "Nothing but could you close the door?"

Dad sends a text to his son: "Your mother has left…"

Son: "OMG. Where did she go?"

Dad: "The shop."

Daughter: "Dad, there is a spider in the bath!"

Dad: "Scare it out with one of your duckface selfies."

Mom: "I just checked the internet history on the computer…"

Dad: "Don't look at me, I look at porn at work."

Son: *"Dad, have you seen my baseball cap?"*

Dad: "I think the real question is: why do you wear one when you don't play the sport?"

Mom: "I can't get the shower to turn off."

Dad: *"Have you tried asking it nicely?"*

Daughter: "Have you seen my skinny jeans?"

Dad: "Why do you need those when you just started wearing elephant pants?"

Son: "Dad, who do you think will win the Super Bowl?

Dad: "The Super Spoon."

Mom: "I invited my mother over for dinner. What should we do?"

Dad: "Play hide and seek."

Dad overhears that his son is going on his first date.

Dad's advice to his son: "If she is pretty, she will leave and it will hurt like hell. But, if she's ugly, she will leave too but you won't care as much."

Daughter: "Do I look good for this interview?"

Dad: "Do you want a rod?"

Daughter: "What? Why?"

Dad: "To help you when you are fishing for compliments."

Mom: "Can you help me open this jar?"

Dad: "Isn't that why you married me?"

Son: "Dad, my gf broke up with me."

Dad: "Did you buy her anything?"

Son: "I got her everything she ever wanted."

Dad: "There's your reason."

Son: "Dad, my wife is having a baby."

Dad: "Finally proof that you like women."

Mom: "Can you go upstairs and check on your son?"

Dad: "No, but I can face-time him instead."

Son: "Dad, what was the first thing mom noticed about you?"

Dad: "The car. It was definitely the car."

Daughter: "I'm taking a shower."

Dad: "Don't forget to bring it back."

Son: "Dad, have you been on my laptop?"

Dad: "No, why?"

Son: "Well, when I opened it I found National Geographic's website."

Dad: "It was your mother."

Mom: "Can you get me some light bulbs from the store?"

Dad: *"Now there's a bright idea."*

Mom: "What's your phone number for work again?"

Dad: *"012345678"*

Mom: "It's not ringing."

Mom: "Why is there a photo of our wedding in the basement?"

Dad: "To scare away the rats dear."

Son: "What's the funniest joke you know?"

Dad: "When you were young and I called you a girl and then you hit me with your handbag."

Son: "Dad, when's dinner?"

Dad: "When your mom comes back."

Dad: "Do you know what I say to your mom before she gets in the car?"

Son: "No, what?"

Dad: "Get in the car."

Daughter to her dad: "What is it?"

Dad: "'It' is a pronoun."

A grumpy Dad goes into his son's room.

Dad: "If you don't add me on Facebook, I'm going to tell your mother..."

Son: "Sure dad, she will be so angry"

Dad quickly replies back: "...tell her how to see the internet history and what you've been looking at."

Dad: "Do you know how to make somebody curious?"

Son: "No, how?"

Dad: "I'll tell you tomorrow."

Mom: "I hate my new haircut."

Dad: "Don't worry. It will grow on you."

How do you make your girlfriend love you?

Tell her you got paid.

Son is sitting next to his dad and says "I think the greatest thing is falling asleep on the couch here and waking up with a blanket."

Dad: "Sure, unless you live alone."

Dad: "Why did you delete me off Facebook?"

Son: "Every picture of me skateboarding has a comment from you saying 'Wear a helmet."

Mom: "The bath is running upstairs."

Dad: "Why aren't you chasing it?"

Mom: "I got a special treat for you tonight."

Dad: "Oh, are you going to bingo?"

I met your mother at the laundromat; she was impressed that I could do my own laundry.

Son: "Do you have an encyclopedia around?"

Dad: "Just ask your mother. She knows everything!"

Son: "Dad, I am thinking about popping the question?"

Dad: "Oh yeah?"

Son: "Where should I take her?"

Dad: "Well, if you take her to a fancy restaurant she will expect it. So maybe take her to the last place she would expect you to take her"

Son: "Oh, where's that?"

Dad: "A fancy restaurant."

What's the biggest difference between your mom and my job?

After 20 years, my job still blows.

Dad to son: "Do you want to go fishing?"

Son: "Hell yeah!"

Dad: "Great! Fish me a beer from the cooler."

Son: "What's the best way to get promoted at work?"

Dad: "With a straw"

Son: "What?"

Dad "When you start sucking ass"

A girl is getting ready to go to her prom. "Dad could you pin this flower on me?"

Dad replies excitedly "Sure. I love pin the tail on the donkey."

A family is at a restaurant when the waiter appears. The dad asks "What's the special?"

Waiter replies "The seafood platter."

Dad then remarks "Sounds fishy. Might make me feel eel."

Mom started a diet that involved a lot of tropical fruit; dad walks into the kitchen and has a look around.

Dad: "There is so much fruit here; it's enough to make a mango crazy."

Dad bursts into his son's room one morning and does a Chewbacca impression. Son asks "What was that about".

Dad: "I wanted to see if you were ewok"

Dad asks his son: "I know you took my playboys from under my bed and I'm disappointed."

Son: "Oh, sorry dad."

Dad: "Why didn't you use the internet instead?"

It's Chloe's 18th birthday in a week. She asks her dad how she would make the party space themed.

Dad replies: "You planet."

Dad is cleaning the house with the vacuum. He turns to mom and says "I think we should sell this. It sucks!"

A family is going on a picnic when they notice that mom forget to bring pickles.

Dad, looking a bit frustrated says "You forgot the pickles. It's kind of a big dill."

Son: "Dad, when do you know you are a man?"

Dad: "The day you have to wash your own clothes."

Daughter looking in mirror: "I have such dry skin."

Dad: "Oh, well the leading cause for that is a towel."

Son: "I want to study archaeology."

Dad: "Your whole career will be in ruins!!"

Son: "Dad, what's the best way to ask out a girl?"

Dad: "By asking her out."

Son: "What do you remember the most about your wedding?"

Dad: "Well, it was so beautiful that even the cake was in tiers."

Chapter Two
Kid Jokes

Why do clowns have big red noses?

I don't know either. I tried to check on Wikipedia, but Wi-Fi is down.

The cat got kitty litter everywhere.

It was a cat-astrophe.

I stood on the cat's tail.

He said me-owww!

What did the cat say to the dog?

Nothing. They can't talk.

How do you get a hippo into bed?

Piece of cake.

How do you get a frog off a tree?

Rip-it.

Did you hear about the horse that was in an accident?

It's now in a stable condition.

What do Eminem and a snake have in common?

They know how to rap.

How does the ocean say hello to you?

It waves.

Son: "What's the worst thing about school?"

Dad: "That you are only there for 8 hours and not more."

When can elephants swim?

When they use their trunks.

Why does Batman hate Superman?

Because he can fly.

What country in the world has the most fish?

Cod-anda

What do a chicken and an ostrich have in common?

Quite a lot actually.

Why do people like to sing in the shower?

Because it's the safest place from harsh criticism and judgement.

When's the best day to ask someone to buy you ice-cream?

Sundae.

What animal can't fly, swim, or run very fast?

Your mom.

What should you always say to grandma after she gives you a present?

Did you keep the receipt?

Did you hear about the dog magician?

He disappeared with a woof.

I am scared of elevators, so I'm taking steps to avoid them.

Why do octopuses win fights?

They are well-armed.

Why was the tree afraid of the dog?

Because he had a little bark.

What time do alligators go to sleep?

12 o'crock.

What's the most musical planet in space?

Nep-tune.

What planet has the biggest butt?

Uranus.

Dad: "Doctor, can I play the trumpet after I heal?"

Doctor: "Yes."

Dad: "Great. I never could before."

What do fishermen do when they are bored?

Play go fish.

Dad looking at a pumpkin: "This is gourd-geous!"

Why is math so hard?

Because there are so many problems.

Why do kids bring calculators to church?

To count their blessings.

Why was the boy bringing a ladder to the pool?

So he could do a high dive.

How does a teacher control her students these days?

By threatening to follow them on social media.

Why does the teacher wear sunglasses inside?

Because her students are always taking selfies.

How do you play a drum?

With a beat.

How do you know when your tiger isn't hungry?

He stops trying to eat you.

What's long and brown and sticky?

A stick.

Where does the spider read the news?

On the web.

How did the boy play catch?

With a ball.

What did the girl do when she woke up?

She had breakfast.

Why do kids love teddys so much?

Because they are can take a punch.

What's the worst thing about being a grapefruit?

That you look nothing like a grape.

How do you make someone laugh in school?

Show them the lunch you made yourself.

Why did the magnet date the other magnet?

They were attracted to each other.

What do you call a fat Pokémon?

Whatever you want. They can't chase you.

Why did Pikachu go to the bathroom?

He needed to squirtle.

How do you annoy your friend?

How do you annoy your friend?

How do you annoy your friend?

How do you annoy your friend?

What does a witch do for fun?

Makes gingerbread men.

I went to the zoo but I left. It was full of animals...

What did the Hulk say to Iron Man?

Not a lot. He doesn't talk much.

Dad: "Do you know why the dog has a human name?"

Son: "no, why?"

Dad: "So I can talk about her achievements more than yours."

Do you know where I hide your xmas presents?

In your laundry basket.

What's a pigs favorite dance?

The fox-trot.

What's the best way to wax a car?

With a candle.

What did one lawyer say to the other?

We are both lawyers.

How do you know when a clock is hungry?

It goes back four seconds.

Did you hear about the invention of the wheel?

It caused a revolution.

How do you keep someone in suspense......?

Chapter Three
The World around Us

Why are so many of the best athletes from Africa?

Because they probably don't own a TV.

Son catches dad watching a YouTube video about Minecraft.

Son: "Dad, what are you watching?"

Dad: "I thought it was a Disney movie but the graphics are awful."

Dad: "Why do so many people send eggplant emojis online?"

Son: "That usually means penis"

Dad: "Oh no! I thought it meant like hello. I sent one to my boss."

Dad goes to a coffee shop: "Can I get an Americano?"

Barista: "Sure. I will write your name on it and shout it when it's ready."

Dad: "Call me 'the greatest dad in the world.'"

Barista: "How about no."

Dad: "Fine, just call me 'plain old boring dad.'"

A dad and his son are driving down a road.

Son: "Look at all the cows over in that field"

Dad: "I will look at some of them, ok."

Son: "Did you try to delete some photos off Facebook?"

Dad: "Yea, how did you know?"

Son: "Well, you wrote delete under them."

Dad: "I got tickets for you to see Bon Jovi."

Mom: "Oh, when are we going?"

Dad: "You are going next week."

Dad opens the fridge and looks confused.

Dad: "What's this crap?"

Daughter: "It's called hummus."

Dad: "What did I tell you about putting dog food in the fridge?"

Dad is sat on the couch watching fox news.

Daughter: "You shouldn't watch that; it's lots of misinformation."

Dad: "But you spend hours reading nonsense on Facebook."

Dad goes into a supermarket.

Clerk: "Do you want this milk in a bag?"

Dad: "Yes, otherwise it will go all over the place."

Mom: "Valentines is around the corner, got anything planned?"

Dad: "It's on a Wednesday so I'll be at work."

A couple of trick or treaters knock on the door on Halloween.

Dad opens door: "Oh, thank god, I thought you were Mormons."

Dad is taking the dog for a walk around the park.

Old lady: "Your dog is scaring away the pigeons."

Dad: "You are mistaken. He's trying to save you from those vultures."

Son: "Can you help me with my English homework?"

Dad: "Why? Are you going to England?"

What's the best way to make a Canadian apologize?

Step on their foot.

Dad is taking the dog for a walk around the park.

Old lady: "Your dog is scaring away the pigeons."

Dad: "You are mistaken. He's trying to save you from those vultures."

Son: "Can you help me with my English homework?"

Dad: "Why? Are you going to England?"

Son: "I'm going to order some Chinese food. Do you want some?

Dad: "I will stick to traditional American food like burritos."

What is Syria's national bird?

Duck

I asked my North Korean friend how he was.

He said he can't complain.

How do you make a German angry?

Tell them you hate sausages.

What's fat and lives in Poland?

A fat pole.

How do you make French people smile?

With wine and cheese.

What do you call a Mexican without a car?

A guy without a car.

Where's the worst place to live in the world?

No idea. Can you check on Google?

Dad: "What's this Zumba class about?"

Mom: "It's a dance work-out."

Dad: "Oh wow, and you don't need wine to dance either huh?"

Dad: "I can't believe that there are people on the internet arguing about silly things."

Mom: "Where have you been for the last 15 mins?"

Dad: "Winning an argument on Facebook."

Dad: "Do you know what the fastest country in the world is?"

Son: "Nope."

Dad: "Rush-a."

Dad is walking through Walmart when he sees a morbidly obese person on a scooter.

Dad: "Look at that. I came to here to buy red bull not see them."

My dad is so offensive. The other day at dinner he called my girlfriend a sheep because she is a vegan. She said she felt so baaaaaad.

Dad: "what's your latest fb post about?"

Daughter: "The diversity of genders. That there are more than 2 genders in the world."

Dad: "I didn't know that. I guess now I'm trans-parent about the topic."

Dad to mom: "Hey let's go to Cuba. It looks like everyone there is Havana good time"

Dad is talking to mom about their next holiday, and says "Let's go to Switzerland. The flag is a big plus."

Mom starts to sigh, but then Dad says "Ok, maybe Moscow, but we shouldn't be Russian things."

What's a French person's favorite video game?

Wii

Son is working on an assignment and decides to ask his dad for help.

Son: "Dad, do you know anything about the Dead Sea?"

Dad: "I had no idea it was sick."

Mom is writing a resume on her laptop when she needs help saving the file. Dad shows up to help.

Dad: "Highlight all the work and then press the deliver button. It says 'del' on it."

Daughter: "Dad, I'm vegetarian now."

Dad: "So, does that mean are you going to marry a carrot?"

Son: "Do you know where the English Channel is?"

Dad: "It's not on this TV, I can tell you that much."

Chapter Four
Insult Jokes

Son: "Do you know how to paint the wall? I've tried to but I think there's some technique."

Dad: "I guess it's time I told you that you were dropped as a child."

Son: "Where do you put the rubbish for recycling?"

Dad: "Oh, you aren't putting it under your bed this month?"

Son: "Why can't I find my wallet?"

Dad: "No idea but I think I've seen your purse in the kitchen."

Son: "Erm, I think the toilet is blocked"

Dad: "And you don't have the mental capacity to fix it so you are telling me now?"

Son: "Should I save money for a car?"

Dad: "What's the point? You would only waste your money on a girlfriend anyways."

Son: "Can I borrow your car tonight?"

Dad: "No way. You can't even wear matching socks."

Son: "Dad, what should I get mom for her birthday?"

Dad: "Go to the attic for inspiration."

Son: "Did I hear you singing in the shower this morning?"

Dad: "Did I hear you moaning in your room last night?"

Son: "Have you fed the dog?"

Dad: "No, but I fed the family of rats living under your bed."

Son: "I have a dance next week but have no moves. Can you show me how to dance?"

Dad: "The cat chasing a torch has a better chance at dancing than you."

Son: "You are starting to go bald."

Dad: "I'd rather be bald than have a face that resembles a pizza."

Son: "I can see your gut."

Dad: "I can see your stupid face and it's making my eyes bleed."

Son: "I'm bringing my girlfriend over. Try not to embarrass me."

Dad: "Oh you will do that all by yourself, especially when she sees your mess of a room."

Mom: "Don't stay up too late."

Dad: "I won't. Hopefully I get into bed just before you start snoring."

Son: "The dog is outside, so who will you blame for your farts now?"

Dad: "I'll tell people it's your breath."

Son: "I think I might win next week's football game"

Dad: "You talk so much crap that the crap that comes out of your ass is better quality."

Son: "Am I adopted?"

Dad: "Not yet. It seems nobody is interested but you can keep hoping."

Angry daughter: "Kiss my ass!"

Dad: "Not until you shave it."

Son: "Dad, you need to turn the TV down."

Dad: "If I wanted to hear from a butthole, I'd just fart."

Chapter Five
Old Age

My last chance to have a smoking hot body is cremation.

Son: "Why did you start jogging?"

Dad: "So I could hear heavy breathing again."

Dad looking over at his son on the couch: "Never underestimate the power of a nap son. They can prevent old age, especially while driving."

I hate trying to read playboy at my age. There are just not enough articles to read.

Dad after doing a stretch: "My back goes out more than I do."

Dad to son: "Enjoy your hair while you still have it."

Son, at my age flowers scare the hell out of me.

I don't want a birthday cake this year. I know the candles will cost more than the cake.

Dad: "What's that drivel music you listen to?"

Son: "It's called hip-hop."

Dad: "More like shit-hop."

I hate it when strangers open the door for me; I know how to use one.

I tried going to the gym but by the time I put on my gym gear in the changing room, everything was closed.

The great thing about being old is there is no more peer pressure.

Dad: "What does LMAO mean in a text?"

Son: "Laughing my ass off."

Dad: "Oh, that might actually happen."

Dad: "Just watched an interesting documentary about beavers."

Son: "Oh?"

Dad: "It was the best damn program I've ever seen."

Dad: "Son, help me wash my car and you can have $5."

Son: "No, I will do it for free."

Dad: "Good, because I don't have $5."

Sometimes when I buy wine, I stand at the register a bit longer than normal hoping that the cashier asks for ID.

Chapter Six
Quick off the Mark

Delivery guy: "Can you sign for this package?"

Dad: "Another day, another autograph."

Son: "Dad, what is the capitol of Ireland?"

Dad: "I."

Son: "Dad, can you teach me to shave my face?"

Dad: "Ask your mom."

Waitress: "Is there anything else I can get you?"

Dad: "Someone to pay the bill."

Waitress: "Careful, this plate is very hot."

Dad: "That's ok, so am I."

Son: "Hey dad, did you get a haircut?"

Dad: "I got them all cut actually."

Daughter: "How do I look?"

Dad: "By using your eyes."

Son: "Hey Dad, what's up?"

Dad: "The ceiling and sky."

Dad: "Bring me a bucket."

Son: "Why?"

Dad: "So I can show you a bucket."

Dad: "Bring me my thinking hat."

Son: "Which hat is that?"

Dad: "The one that says the 'Greatest Dad in the World.'"

Daughter brings her new boyfriend to the house.

Dad: "Are you going to take my daughter away?"

Date: "Oh no sir."

Dad: "That's a shame."

Bonus Dad Jokes

Daughter: "Hmm, I don't seem to be in any of my friend's group photos."

Dad: "That's cause you're ugly."

Son: "Dad, my head hurts."

Dad: "My head would hurt too if it was that big."

Mom: "Does this dress make me look fat?"

Dad: "Do you mean fat horizontally or fat vertically?"

Daughter: "I'm going to start a diet."

Dad: "Oh really, I guess I can tell you where I hid all the cookies then?"

Son: "Dad, please make me a bagel?"

Dad: "Ok. Abra kadabra, you are now a bagel!"

Son: "Dad, Mom can't find her phone. Can you call it?"

Dad: "No problem. Mom's phone! Mom's phone!"

Daughter is getting ready for work: "Dad what time is it now?"

Dad shouts back: "I don't know, it keeps changing."

Son: "Could you call me a taxi, please?"

Dad: "As you wish, dear taxi."

Son: "Dad, I'm dating a girl but she's very short"

Dad: "Better short than not a tall."

Son: "Where's the bin?"

Dad: "I haven't been anywhere!"

Mom: "Can you take out the rubbish now?"

Dad "I can't, my favorite commercial is on."

Daughter: "Dad, did you just fart?"

Dad: "Yes, to make you smell better."

Daughter: "Dad, I'm going to the zoo."

Dad: "Great. Bring your mom, she likes to play with tigers."

Son: "Ah, I just stubbed my toe."

Dad: "Do you want me to call the toe truck?"

Nurse: "Do you smoke?"

Dad: "Only when I'm on fire."

Waitress: "Sorry about your wait."

Dad: "Well, I have been trying to lose a few pounds before swimsuit season.

How many times did you laugh?

I hope it was over 100 times.

If you did, then I'd really appreciate it if you would post a short review on Amazon.

Just let me know which joke or jokes you enjoyed the most? 😊

I read all the reviews myself so that I can continue to provide joke books that people want.

Please visit the link below which will redirect you to my Amazon author page, then select this book, scroll down and leave your review.

www.MikeGaffyBooks.com

Thanks for your support!

Bonus!

Get This Free Joke Book!
Hilarious jokes to make you laugh your head off!
Visit The Link Below!

www.SavageJokes.com

Made in the USA
Lexington, KY
24 November 2018